T0380474

Kisses Kindling

Jarrette Fellows Jr.

Copyright © 2021 Jarrette Fellows Jr.

All rights reserved. No part of this book may be used or reproduced by any means, graphic, electronic, or mechanical, including photocopying, recording, taping or by any information storage retrieval system without the written permission of the author except in the case of brief quotations embodied in critical articles and reviews.

Archway Publishing books may be ordered through booksellers or by contacting:

Archway Publishing
1663 Liberty Drive
Bloomington, IN 47403
www.archwaypublishing.com
844-669-3957

Because of the dynamic nature of the Internet, any web addresses or links contained in this book may have changed since publication and may no longer be valid. The views expressed in this work are solely those of the author and do not necessarily reflect the views of the publisher, and the publisher hereby disclaims any responsibility for them.

Any people depicted in stock imagery provided by Depositphotos are models, and such images are being used for illustrative purposes only. Certain stock imagery © Depositphotos.

Scripture quotations marked KJV are from the Holy Bible, King James Version (Authorized Version). First published in 1611. Quoted from the KJV Classic Reference Bible, Copyright © 1983 by The Zondervan Corporation.

ISBN: 978-1-6657-0132-7 (sc)
ISBN: 978-1-6657-0133-4 (hc)
ISBN: 978-1-6657-0134-1 (e)

Library of Congress Control Number: 2021900354

Print information available on the last page.

Archway Publishing rev. date: 2/19/2021

1 Corinthians 7:1–5

Nevertheless, to avoid fornication, let every man have his own
wife, and let every woman have her own husband.

Let the husband render to the wife due affection: and
likewise also the wife unto the husband.

The wife hath not the power of her own body, but the husband; and likewise
the husband hath not the power of his own body, but the wife.

Deprive ye not one the other, except it be with consent for a time, that
ye may give yourselves to fasting and prayer; and come together again,
that the enemy tempt you not because of lack of self-control.

To my wife, Vivian, for whom my love is everlasting.

Double-X-rated gourmet smooches and warm, romantic prose for the men who seek the path to fiery romance and their women who long for more.

Penned with a culinary motif because the best kisses always taste good.

The lovelorn know that love tames a bad-tempered woman and the male savage beast.

Contents

Kisses Kindling

Twelve Gourmet Smooches for Husband and Wife

1. Honey-Lemon
Wakeup greeting before the coffee. Intensity: 2.0

2. Suga Cookie
Off to work. Intensity: 3.0

3. Strawberry Charm
Anytime with sweet platitudes. Intensity: 7.0

4. Passionfruit
Rekindling the passion. Intensity: 7.5

5. Cherry Jubilee
Affirming the love. Intensity: 8.0

6. Sweet Brownie
Stoking the flames. Intensity: 8.5

7. Plum Delightful
Sunset ecstasy. Intensity: 9.0

8. Sugar Peach
Sweetly erotic. Intensity: 10.5

9. Midnight Honey
Passion under cover. Intensity: 12.0

10. My Moonlight Sonata
For the smitten. Intensity: 14.0

11. Steamy Body
Steamy love. Intensity: 16.0

12. Amour Volcanique
Not for the coy. Intensity: Off the Charts

Love Makes a Man Gentle

Once, there was a time when I was
incapable of fully appreciating the
remarkable sanctity of a woman.
Apart from simply not knowing how,
neither had I the emotional maturity
to comprehend your depth, for you
are not formed of shallow substance.

But because of you, my former self is of
a bygone time. You are special, having
refined me and driven away that callous
man. I can now be intimate. You are my
fragrant flower, symbolizing the women who
yearn for sensitivity. Love makes a man gentle.

You are my gift to love and behold.
Love makes a man gentle.

While unregenerate, I was a rock
void of understanding. I thought of
you as a strange thing, hopelessly
consigned to some Adamic curse.

From that came wisdom.
Unwieldy machismo erodes the
male mind like a driving rain turns
the earth to mush.

But that is the past. Your
novelty is not oddity or idiosyncrasy.
You are a gift, not a burden. To love
a woman like you is an answer to prayer,
for to love profoundly is no simple thing.
Its temperature will not soon decline.

I know it enriches your soul
and makes you glad.
Love makes me gentle.

The grandness of love and its beauty
say to us that the depth of our romantic
furlough can extend as deeply as
our passionate designs.

If not for your appearing, I would have
never realized my potential to love a
woman the way I love you. You lighten
my gait and make my rough surface smooth.

You have increased my understanding
of a woman—your need for intimacy,
for affection over primal lust, a sensitive
ear over the arrogance of machismo.
Love makes a man gentle.

I am hypnotized by your allure,
eloquence, and radiance—the essence
of inner and outer beauty, a
wonderful example of a woman.

To embrace you is a call to
my heart. You fill me with zeal.
Love makes a man gentle.

A new day is another opportunity to renew our love.

Romance's Fire

The kindling for romance is imagination.
Creative cultivation always engenders
the tingling heat of romance.

Romance's fire is not only for newfound love;
it provides warm oil to creaky, time-worn
marriages, too—those that have stood the
test of many years that tell us matrimony
can be forever.

An old man may not be able to carry his damsel
over the threshold anymore, but romance's
fire can restore crackling joy to his soul and
loving appreciation to hers.

It can rebuke any frigid encroachment by
apathy to chill the love that always burns hot
in the beginning. Romance's fire keeps love alive
because it is unquenchable when the flames
are fanned.

To fan the flames merely requires a little
imagination. But use with caution, for
romance's fire is potent.

There are many inducements to tend the
flames. The gift of a diamond may light the
fuse; a bouquet of flowers can engender a rush
of passion; hoping for romance on soft green
earth beneath a star-ladened night sky
can bring it about in nice order too.

But to enkindle a much hotter flame
and a completely bliss-filled conflagration,
nothing infuses romance's fire quite like a kiss.

Husband and wife ably using
their imaginative powers can create
a multitude of impassioned kisses.

Men, expand your creative inclinations.
Exhilarate her; make her giggle wildly.
Your marriage will love it,
and you will love your marriage.

It begins with a kiss.

Honey-Lemon

Special Allurements
Bouquet of yellow zinnias
Fresh lemon wedges

This kiss represents the least potent kiss and usually occurs just after the night's snooze before the coffee. You kiss her to remind her that you love her as much as yesterday.

Honey-lemon represents a soft touch, like the sweet morning dew and the glint of the morning sunrise. It is like the easy new dawn filled with an avian symphony and a cool breeze gently flowing through the trees. Honey-lemon is resplendent and fresh, symbolic of all the hope that a new day brings.

Purchase the yellow zinnias the day before to have available for the morning.

To make this kiss titillating, squeeze lemon drops on her ear, and then gently lick before moving to her lips for a prolonged smooch.

Intensity: 2.0

This simple kiss can be hot honey-lemon as well and register beyond 5.0 on the intensity scale.

When this occurs, often it is due to frosty, wintry conditions on a Saturday morn when the warmth of the bedcovers sends a tantalizingly tempting refrain: remain beneath the covers.

Suga Cookie

Special Allurements
Mouthwash

This kiss happens just before you push off to work or before you go your separate ways. Suga cookie sets the tone for the day. A sweet peck on the pucker is wonderful; a little suga goes a long way because suga is stronger than caffeine, a better pickup than an espresso, and absolutely calorie-free.

Suga cookie will last the day long, inducing fleeting flashbacks of your lover's lips, eyes, nose, and other unnamed parts—a tender reminder that you're never alone.

Intensity: 3.0

Strawberry Charm

Special Allurements
Strawberries in season, chilled
Bouquet of red camellias
Strawberry-scented candle

This kiss can happen anytime, but nighttime is best to communicate sweet platitudes saying, "I love you!"

Before you arrive home, stop by the florist for a bouquet of red camellias. Purchase fresh strawberries in season; chill in a silver-plated dish before bedtime.

A couple of hours after dinner, retrieve the strawberries, take her hand, and head for the bedroom. Light the candle; place near the red camellias. Slide into silken pajamas; splash on cologne. Turn the lights low. Put on some mood music.

Take a chilled strawberry, and place it into your lady's mouth. Place one in your mouth too, enjoying the succulence together, symbolizing sweet ecstasy.

Share the symbolism of the red camellias—that she is a flame in your heart and you have never been more deeply in love with her. Whisper it over and over.

Lick her neck, blow into her ear, and caress her spine. Embrace and kiss her like it is the first time. Then let your romantic inclinations run wild.

Intensity: 7.0

Arctic Season

When the sun shines in our relationship
like sparkling gold, our union is golden. Even
so, we are ever perfecting it, and sometimes an
arctic wind does intrude, chilling our bond,
making our love shiver.

It only makes our bond stronger because
the sunshine always returns, reminding us of our
blessed union when it enters our relationship
like sparking gold.

Our union is golden.

A *real* man is genteel. You delight
not in bruising your queen's emotions
because you are the stronger. When bearish
instincts do take rule over you momentarily,
you know how to abase yourself, crucify
your ego, and soothe her tender heart.

Machismo accomplishes nothing. Need the
lion debate with the wildebeest? Elephant
with the mole? Eagle with the sparrow?

You need cherish and care for your queen
who was a good thing when your emotions
first embraced, never to be put asunder.

The man who stumbles craves forgiveness
and provides emotional ointment for her ravages.
Only then will you again taste the nectar of her
love, sealed by the privilege of a kiss.

Passionfruit

Special Allurements
Passionfruit in season
Bouquet of primrose
Apple cinnamon-scented candle

Now is the time to kiss and make up. But sir, you must
first rekindle the passion. You can do it!

Remember your first argument? She wept outwardly, and you wept inwardly. You
never felt so badly. You were in love with her with all your heart, and you never
really meant to hurt her. You wanted to make amends like there was no tomorrow.

You assured her everything would be all right—and it was. Now you must do it again.

Secure a cabin for the weekend. Purchase a crystal vase, and fill it with a bouquet of red
primrose. The cabin must have a woodburning fireplace. Bring your own scented logs,
a favorite Chablis, some chocolate kisses, and your most titillating cologne and perfume.

Pack your softest cotton PJs, but make sure she packs her scanty
red or pink lingerie. Reserve it all for the first night.

After some quiet talk before the crackling wood fire and
some gentle touching and caressing, retire to bed.

Our love grows richer with the passing of time.

Don't forget the passionfruit, bouquet of red primrose, and the scented candles.

With the scented candle ushering in the mood, hopefully winter's snow has chilled the night air and a starry sky shimmers through your bedroom skylight.

Snuggle up, and tell your lady the beautiful red primrose is symbolic—that you cannot live without her and are passionately in love. Augment that theme; share a little passionfruit with arms interlocked.

Slip beneath the wool blankets and silky sheets. The feeling is majestic, fit for king and queen. Take the lead, kind sir. The bed is undefiled, and you belong to each another.

Your emotions are surging now—testosterone level percolating with glee.

Pull her close. Imagination reigns.

Intensity: 7.5

Like snowflakes falling softly from heaven, I have again fallen in love with you.

Wild Cherry

Special Allurements
Cherries in season, chilled
Bouquet of hydrangea
Wild cherry-scented candle

Now has come the morning. The night outside your cabin was frigid, but indoors, cozy warmth remains as the fireplace crackles and pops with soothing heat. As the two of you awaken, you gently stroke and massage her body, still aromatic from the perfume bath of the foregone night. Your body too still emanates a powerful allure.

Now it's time to reaffirm last night's passion. But first, you slip out of bed to retrieve the chilled cherries for a time such as this. Delicately kiss your love, and allow the smooch to linger. This is delicious, and who's in a hurry, anyway? Place a sweet, succulent cherry into her mouth. Allow her to return the favor. Repeat to build up a reserve of energy.

Tell your lady the bouquet of hydrangea symbolizes your heartfelt bond to her. Fondle and caress for extended moments. Stoke the passion till molten, but stop short of eruption. Monsieur, *s'il vous plait,* now is the time to kiss her with vigor as the French do.

Fan the fire. Take her higher than the tenth cloud.

Intensity: 8.0

Sweet remembrance means through storms, rain,
laughter, and pain, our love will remain.

Because I Am Mortal

If you and I are flowers growing side by side,
it is not my desire to grow superior and
stunt your growth; I do want to share the
sun, earth, wind, and rain.

And if my petal should overshadow your petal,
nudge me, and I will humbly move it away.
I am a vulnerable flower with mortal
frailties, and should I find damage during
my growth, fall limp, and wither,
I ask only this:

that you nurture my roots,
soothe my weakened stem,
and believe in me, that
I will regain my strong posture
to again reach for the sky.

Cementing the Bond

Birds chirping sweetly say it's time to peel
the covers for a sensuous warm shower.
Temper the water, sir; let it build steam
like you did when you were courting.

Lather her ever so gently. Embrace
and squeal at the supple, slippery eroticism.
Remember how it began? She was the
world to you—your all and everything.
She was your queen.
You still feel that way.

It's good to get away to rediscover
one another, if only to look into one
another's eyes the way you used to.
Holding hands, strolling around the
lake reminds you of the time when you
loved her so much you couldn't eat,
couldn't concentrate on anything
else except her.

That time is now.

Sweet Brownie

Special Allurements
Chocolate brownies
Bouquet of chocolate daffodils
Chocolate-scented candle

Every marriage requires effort to keep romance's fire burning. That means stoking the flames. Nothing should ever be taken for granted.

Romance is a splendored thing not to be taken lightly. It is a gift between two lovers the way God intended. The husband satisfies the wife; the wife reciprocates.

Sir, you did it with aplomb during courtship. You always knew what to say and when to say it. Do it again to stoke a hotter flame. Romance's fire is in your heart. It should never flicker.

Stoke the mood with chocolate-scented candles and a bouquet of daffodils, which symbolize unrequited love. Your lady is the only one for you. The sun always shines in your heart when she's with you. Tell her that. Your love is eternal.

She's the only woman for you.

You may be in snug comfort on a comfortable chaise lounge beneath a giant throw blanket, taking in a video on the big screen.

But there's more to the moment than the movie. Your libido tells you so. Sweet brownie is an after-dinner kiss—a very amorous dessert.

You are ready for hot, tingling amour. Kiss the inside of your lover's ankle, then go high to lick her neck, then keep tasting one another's goodness … slowly, gingerly.

Intensity: 8.5

The love between us has come full bloom, and because it
must never wither, I propose this prayer for two:

Let our passion never simmer, our hearts never fail, our flame burn unto eternity.

Cup for Two

Pour a cup of hot emotion,
stir in a teaspoon of sweet tidings,
add a few drops of lust,
stir vigorously with love.
Savor while hot.

Plum Delight

Special Allurements
Plums in season, halved and cored
Bouquet of blue violets
Plum-scented candle

This kiss is like a perfectly ripe plum—delicately sweet from careful maturation. For couples in love, it is ecstasy unencumbered.

If kids are in the equation, for the right mood, elicit the support of a sitter. The home environment can be ideal, but for more intimacy, reserve a hotel room for the evening. Setting aside special time like this will preserve your marriage and keep love alive and percolating.

Take to the market for a pound of sweet gourmet plums. Halve, core, then chill in the fridge. Visit the florist for a bouquet of blue violets, which symbolize faithfulness— that you will always be true. This will warm her heart with loving reassurance.

Plum-scented candles will add the final touch.

Now, for the setting. Whether in a hotel room or your home's bedroom, light several scented candles, and enhance the mood with some alluring music that underscores the evening's theme.

Sniff the scent of the violets; discuss their floral meaning: always true. The plums will induce quick energy and sweeten the moment.

This is the perfect complement to a romantic dinner for two as both of you share intimate moments about your union and the special love that has so wonderfully cemented your bond.

Dim the lights, but not so low that you cannot see the twinkle in her eyes.

Slip beneath the bedcovers, and shed your silk PJs. Pull your honey close, caressing her gently wherever you decide.

No time for talking—your communication is lip-to-lip, limited only by your romantic creativity.

Never hurry. Savor the moment.

Intensity: 9.0

Sugar Peach

Special Allurements
Peaches in season, halved
Bouquet of orange blossoms
Scented bath oil
Jasmine-scented candles

Orange blossoms, two perfectly round peaches, and jasmine-scented
candles set the tone for the sweetly erotic sugar peach.

Orange blossoms tell your queen that love and marriage between the two
of you is eternal and that your union will bear much fruitfulness.

The setting for this kiss can be at home or in a hotel room.
Privacy is a must—no distractions. Your love deserves all of your
time. These are royal moments not to be taken lightly.

With the scent of jasmine wafting throughout your private
space, accented by mood music, take a slice of peach, and place
it in your lover's mouth. Have her return the favor.

While savoring the fruit, kiss for an extended moment. Dim the lights, and undress.
Rub fragrant bath oil into your palms and rub liberally on one another until silky.

Engage in foreplay. Join lips, licking to tickle, and then lick inside
the ear. What you do next should be sweeter than the fruit.

Intensity: 10.5

Had I the power, I'd reach into the heavens to give
you a star for being the star of my life.

Midnight Honey

Special Allurements
Dollop of honey
Bouquet of gardenias
Apple cinnamon-scented candle

This kiss is definitely passion under the covers. You're secret lovers all over again, like it was in the beginning when your love was your secret. You'd share intimate thoughts for hours—moments you never wanted to end.

But before the coming night's passion, take her back in time. Revisit one of those secret places for nostalgia's sake. Remember that first kiss? You trembled when your lips met for the first time—that's how special it was.

Press your lips together like it's the first time. Relish the moment.

Get ready for the night.

With scented candles burning, tell your queen that the bouquet of gardenias accents the fantasy that you are secret lovers for the night. No one else knows.

Your lady is sweet, but you sweeten her even more with a taste of honey, delicately placing your honey-laden index finger on her tongue. She returns the favor. That deserves a kiss, and you do it the *French* way.

Now, you're tingling from the top of your head to your toes.
You desire her deeply; she desires you deeply.

The bed awaits your undefiled pleasure. Silk pajamas and sheets serve a special allure. Your body fragrances are magnetizing, quickening your heartbeat, inducing a rush of adrenaline. Your body rages for hers, but slow down, sir— never rush. Calm your libido; you want to extend the passion on this night.

For this kiss, midnight is absolutely best. Embrace, and allow the silkiness in the PJs to ravish you. Your skin beneath the garments feels supple and tingly. You feel more alive now than ever before.

Shed the PJs, and massage one another all over. Kiss your love behind her ear, on the tip of her nose, and wherever else you desire. Every inch of her belongs to you—and you to her.

Pace yourselves, and midnight honey will extend well past midnight.

Intensity: 12.0

Words can only express but never fully convey how profound my love is for you.

My Moonlight Sonata

Special Allurements
Bouquet of red roses
Bottle of red Chablis
Two crystal wine glasses

The night lake beneath a silvery moon offers sheer enchantment for the hopelessly smitten. Rays of the moonlight reflect the still lake the way we reflect one another.

Like the courtship of moon and lake, ours is otherworldly, fashioned from On High.

Amid a warm summer breeze this night, I take you in my arms, and
we frolic like newlyweds entangled in bliss all over one another.
We embrace and kiss. What follows exceeds erotic rage!

Intensity: 14.0

Steamy Body

Special Allurements
Dollop of honey
Bouquet of blood red roses
French vanilla-scented candle

Present your queen with a lavish bouquet of blood red roses. This speaks love in the strongest terms, symbolizing your profound love for her.

Enter a hot jacuzzi or steamy shower. Shed the threads, because steamy body is best flesh-to-flesh. Remember "Bone of my bone, flesh of my flesh"? There is no better time to affirm this.

In the hot tub or shower, take her hand, looking into her eyes: Say, "I love you!" Taste the honey, and follow with a tender kiss, after which you caress her lips. Massage one another, careful not to miss a single spot or curve. The steamy bubbles have made your skin so supple you can't help but allow your fingers to lead the way. You're loving it to the nth degree.

After the tub or shower, enter the bedroom; pat one another dry with soft cotton towels, light the scented candle, and then rub on fragrant body oil, using only your fingertips for extra erotic sensation. Now, kiss her belly button.

What comes next is undercover.

Intensity: 16.0

Wisdom over time: if we desire, our love
will last forever and evermore.

Sweetest Passion

Our love is rekindled each new sunrise like a sauna in the morning
roiling with soothing heat, massaging our bond, making it
supple, responsive, and overflowing with sweet passion.

Amour Volcanique

Special Allurements
Dollop of honey
Bouquet of red tulips
Red cinnamon-scented candle

This royal kiss is certainly not for the coy. Amour volcanique leaves
nothing to be desired, as it is an eruption of eroticism.

Set the tone with a bouquet of red tulips that symbolize you are the perfect lover about
to make a declaration of love. Cinnamon-scented candles add the perfect aromatic
touch. A pink negligee for your queen and your rouge bikini shorts add a fiery touch.

Turn the lights low, and play your favorite mood music for lovemaking. After sharing
some honey and spraying on your most alluring aphrodisiac, slink beneath the covers.

Engage in spirited foreplay for the moment. Though you may be ready to
meld, forestall a few moments more. Fan the flames—slide your finger down
her spine, bite her neck ever so gently, lick the inside of her ear, kiss the
curve of her waist, and slide supple fingers to her most intimate spots.

The moment for deepest lovemaking is now. Kind sir, moan if
you must, growl if you must, but hold nothing back!

Make love over and over and forever because every tender
part of your queen belongs to you, her king.

In marriage, the bed is undefiled.

Intensity: Off the Charts

As a diamond is forever, my love for you is eternal.

My passion for you is rekindled with each new sunrise.

Notes from *Kisses Kindling*

The mission of this book is to rekindle the fire in marriages gone cold, reignite the romance that existed in the beginning, and reaffirm that love can last forever—until death do us part. Commitment makes a strong marriage, and a strong marriage brings happiness.

When marriages go strangely awry, couples committed to the will of God for their lives will find this book a beacon of light to steer them back on course, reaffirming their sacred bond.

Love can last forever!

Author Biography

Jarrette Fellows Jr. has worked for more than four decades as a journalist, editor, and publisher. He holds a bachelor of arts in journalism from California State University, Los Angeles. He is the author of a wide range of articles, stories, features, editorials, and commentaries and also currently publishes two digital-specific newspapers. He currently lives with his family in Los Angeles.

Printed in the United States
By Bookmasters